FAITH, HOPE & LOVE

FolaBim

AuthorHouse™ UK
1663 Liberty Drive
Bloomington, IN 47403 USA
www.authorhouse.co.uk
Phone: 0800.197.4150

This book is printed on acid-free paper.

ISBN: 978-1-7283-9598-2 (sc)
ISBN: 978-1-7283-9597-5 (e)

Print information available on the last page.

Published by AuthorHouse 12/16/2019

authorHOUSE®

FAITH, HOPE & LOVE

CONTENTS

Waving the White Flag

My Maker! My Creator!
Knitted by my confusion
knotted by my frustration,
knowing my desperation!
Waving the White Flag,
I surrender to The Father!
My Saviour! My Lord!
groped by hidden sins,
gripped by guilt within,
grabbed by deep fears,
waving stained White Flag,
I surrender to The Word!
The Blood! His Blood!
Plagued by all pleasures
plunged in luxury leisure's
pushed by lascivious lusts
waving the red White Flag,
I surrender to The Cross.
Holy Spirit! Holy Ghost!
A rubble in the crevice,
rubbish in the bin of life
rough by demonic vice
Waving the ash white Flag!
I surrender to The Fire.
Waving the white flag
I surrender as Daughter!
I surrender as Wife!
I surrender as Mother!
I surrender as Grandma!
My roles, my inner Pride,
Surrender all to Your will!

Waving the white flag,
I surrender as Son!
I surrender as Husband!
I surrender as Father!
I surrender as Grandad!
My roles! My Lion Pride!
Surrender all to Your will!

Paralysed with love

Today I became officially,
Paralysed with your love,
This morn my heart skipped,
irregular beats then stopped!
No appetite for good food,
hungered for your love.
Surely you are my Turtle Dove.
Today I became mindless.
My attitude now reckless!
Strangled the duvet, clueless.
Droplets filled the stale air
Your Spirit hovered in the atmosphere

Like a sponge your presence
Tangible! Terrifying! Yet Tender!
So real! Yes! Utterly unbelievable.
The dead came to visit. Unimaginable!
Our love is alive - that is unfathomable!
Hollywood would say - unfashionable.
No force so graciously great
No power can unite so strong,
Nothing can make it wrong
No diamond ring can hold
No sickness, disease or cold.
Even death cannot dethrone
Where true love condones,
When two flesh becomes one
Herein a gallant victory won.
Today your love waltzed in
hitting like a huge tidal wave.
Sent electrical shocks to my veins

people may call me vain, insane.
Nothing could stop this passion!
No one can uproot this sensation.
Not even death can engulf it!
The grave can only stall it!

Our love union revolves the orbit.
The sun! The moon! The stars!
The Father! The Son! The Spirit!
Rejoices in true love, my dove.
On my date you came from yonder.
Drew me and filled with wonder!

Our Song - Valentine Tribute

Darling, they are playing our song,
Yes my love, That perfect harmony,
Played by the heavenly symphony!
It was our music,
When two hearts pound together in a beat,
Under the sheet,
the sweating heat!
Yelling "Happy Valentine!"
Can you hear my sweet?
Did you get my tweet?
They are playing our song,
Our loving melody
"Endless love"
Can you remember the lyrics?
Can your feet still tap
To the beat?
Sweetheart, can you
remember the fifteen of November?
When we sat entwined at the movies,
Your birthday treat.
We held hands,
like Brookshield and her lover
so clean, so young -
Frolicking in the pool instead of school,
But their love was like our love,
So real, so strong,
Even though families thought it was so wrong!
Dearest, they are playing our song,
Listen to the lyrics

"you are my endless love"
Oh my turtle dove
Can you hear?
Are you there?
I want to shout!
Just want to scream!
Life is but a dream,
This is our song!
This is our dance!
tap, tap, so neat,
on our feet.
When two hearts melts
like Strawberry ice in the summer heat,
My heart skipped two beats,
as you wrapped me in your
"Endless love".
We waltzed, tip-toed,
cheek to cheek swaying
to and fro at the
strumming of the harp strings.
and band of angels sing.
Beloved. Can you remember
that night in November?
No! You cannot hear!
No! You cannot feel!
You are as cold as steel,
I stand over you in my high heels
as you lay perfectly still...
laid in that lonely hill.
Beloved, they are playing our song,
but you are gone,

gone away, far too soon...
Today I am blessed,
because I heard our song,
so pleased to hear that sound,
The Rhythm, the Rhyme,
The high pitch of the sweet Soprano,
that only the two of us knows,
true love is timeless,
from here to eternity,
You will always be "my endless love".
Sleep! Adieu! Farewell!
My soul is well!
Until we meet again
at our Saviour's feet,
Rest in Peace, my dove,
"My endless love"
Yes! We will meet again
loving you was such sweet gain!

My new love: The song of the widow.

Heart shattered like glass!
Mind blinded by confusion,
Life mutilated in desperation
Soul in deep despair depression.
Love gone for a run, strayed!
Family stressed in dismay,
friends, neighbours in disarray!
The cord of suicide on display.
Swimming in muddy miry clay,
sinking, drowning, groaning.
Damaged, destroyed, decaying,
death trolls wilfully, knocking!
Swiftly, His mighty hand stretched,
plunged in, plucked, wrenched me,
yanking my soul, gripped by Sheol!
Uprooted my feet from all evil.
His Light pierced my darkness,
His strength in my weakness,
His love melted my hardness,
His grace relieved my disgrace!
He lifted me high above ground,
setting me upon the Solid Rock,
on Calvary hill, under the cross,
His Blood washed my dross!
In a blink, joy flooded my heart,
grief, mourning and sorrow fled!
Confusion, frustration, degradation,
dissolved, I danced in jubilation.
Who is so strong and mighty?
Who is so awesome yet majestic?
Who can take yet restore life?

Who could heal and deliver?
He is the Wonderful Counsellor!
He is the Invisible God, the Creator!
He is the Man of War, Lord of Hosts!
He is the Stiller of storms, the Restorer.
He is the Husband of the Widow,
He is the Father of the fatherless,
He is the Way, the Truth and the Life!
He is the Author and Finisher of our faith.
He, God, is glorious in Holiness,
He is Redeemer, Teacher and Sustainer.
He is fearful in praises, the Defender
Our Comforter, our Provider, the Potter!
His eyes on me, He let me in,
Graciously, forgave all my sins.
What a Merciful and Gracious God!
What a Mighty and Faithful God!
My Lord! My God! I adore you!
I love you Lord, I worship you!
Now I know the "I AM THAT I AM!"
I surrender to You all that I am!

The HEM of HIS Garment!

Heart pain! heartache! heartburn
Stabbing, digging, piercing,
Sorrow in, sorrow out!
Grief so cruel, nowhere to turn!
Who would assist this heart of mine;
Release the pain that slays!
Must touch the HEM!
Bent treble, bound in fetters,
Invisible chains, hands and feet,
drained of vigour with no favour.
Can't look up, trodden by shame,
Rugged, ridicule, wretched, no fame,
Release this pain of slavery!
Need to touch the HEM!
Looking for love, gentle dove,
another man, another sack!
Divorce, deserted, separated
Depressed, disgruntled, devastated!
Broken, betrayed and battered!
Release this pain that stains!
Gotta touch the HEM!
Hope departed, can't live no more!
Life is a ploy; jesters and jokers,
living in hell, wanting to get well!!
More drugs, more drinks, more fags,
Helpless, hopeless defenceless hags
Release this pain, take the strain
Must touch the HEM!
A distant crowd, shouting, jubilant,
"Touch the HEM; be made whole"
Release the pain that strains!

Jesus is here! Be made whole!
Saw a woman a yonder,
Could not help but wonder,
Drenched in red, should be in bed,
Pushing into the crowd, stretch
forth her weak hands, with all her might,
She touched something, His cloth,
full of glee, her face so bright!
She looked alright, started to flee,
This woman touched the HEM!
The crowd halted! Silent!
"Who touched me" He asks,
A majestic figure, came forth.
Eyes like a river, peace flowing,
Took her hand, lifted her up
"Your faith makes you whole"
Her pain released! Free, no strain!
She touched the HEM!
Throwing out caution, grabbing faith,
It is now! Had no time to wait,
Followed the crowd,pressing in
Reaching out, refusing to doubt.
To touch Him was to be free
Took a chance, stretch out in hope,
Thrusting forward, tip of a finger,
Touched the HEM!
He stopped and gazed at me
"You are free, free indeed!"
"Sins forgiven, a place in heaven"
Pain released, stress and stain,
Electric waves surge into her heart,

New strength out of weakness,
Standing strong,not falling apart.
This is real! This is True!
This is not a show, life made whole.
No more torment, a life spared.
No more delusions! No more fears!
Touched the HEM - JESUS is HERE!

The servant of the I AM

You were His dazzling Light!
Shinning in darkness, His star!
He made you stand, so bright,
with His flames of fire, flickering,
bringing hope without floundering.
He called you as His shepherd,
to share His good news,
Yet, like a helpless moppet,
like a lamb to the slaughter,
Trusting, slain on the altar!
You were sweet, His salt,
Sent to preserve the jobless,
He made you stand as His pillar,
Became taste to the tasteless,
Singing hope to the hopeless.
You were His furnace of fire!
Consuming, engulfing evil lies
His sword sharp in your mouth,
Cutting but giving them new life.
You were sent as His lover,
Comforting, sowing seeds of love,
to family, friends and foes.
You were toast and His host.
You stood your ground,
believing, trusting, caring,
hoping, faithfully awaiting,
patiently, seeking, studying,
praying for His coming!
YES! His second coming.
He led you by His Spirit,
You yielded to His calling,

Refusing to be a Jonah.
Harshly treated like Jeremiah,
He gave you the patience of Job,
To declare to the world - HOPE!
You answered the utmost call,
To break chains, captives free,
To open the eyes, ears and hearts,
To break, down prison doors for all,
Declaring grace, mercy, favour
Pointing to the mighty Saviour.

The Cross of Love - Dedicated for Good Friday

God is awesome Love!
Love gave is only Son,
a perfect, sinless lamb,
Light of the world - our lamp.
Jesus is sacrificial Love
Love went to the Cross
crucified like a game,
Christ bore our shame!
Holy Spirit is solid Love,
Love dwells in the heart,
when we ask Christ in,
He'll forgive all our Sin.
Men needs this Love,
Where is that Love?
It comes from above,
descend like a dove!
Love cries out" Come!"
Love calls from the cross
Repent, all sins forgiven
For man Christ was given!
Love fill soaks the air,
Love covers oceans, seas,
Love permeates the atmosphere
Love dwell on earth - everywhere!
Turn! Turn! Don't miss out!
On your knees, cry, cry aloud!
"Please FORGIVE me! Come abide!
Father, Son, Holy Ghost RESIDE!"

It is like a dream!

It is just a dream, evil dream
You are were the dairy cream
Then, suddenly violently taken,
snatched from the cradle of life.
Just like a dream, weird dream,
You came to the world screaming,
We greeted you with shouts of joy,
Then on rugged table you lay,
for the sake of Christ. they slay
Horrific cries as you fought,
the good fight of faith shouting,
"This my cross to BEAR! My pain"
To live is Christ, to die is gain.
Murderers in white, poisoned in a fight
We cried, pleading, kneeling "Father help!"
Hungry authority snuffled your light!
We stood helpless in death's darkness.
Your beautiful brown eyes turned blue!
It was just a dream! An ugly dream!
Could this be a dream?
This world is not the reality,
In truth, there is eternity!
You love, cherished The Lord
And you whom He so loved,
Lay asleep. deep sweet sleep,
Your blood calls for revenge
Night! Day! Day turned night!
One thing we know, we trust:
The promises are true, right
Where justice reigns, rules!
God rewrite every wrong

Restoring all that was lost
He makes the lame to walk!
Deaf to hear, the blind to see!
With Jesus, lepers are cleansed,
All sickness healed, at ease
With His Word, demons are drivenWe look up, home
is heaven.
Best of all the dead are raised
So in the sweet by and by,
we tweet this happy tune
"Death where is your sting
Grave where is your victory"
God gets all the glory
So sleep on my Cream
Maybe this is a dream!

CHURCH GAMES

Today she heard a voice,
It was so clear as daylight
Gentle as the morning breeze
So soft it made her freeze.
"Come to me, come and rest
Come to me, rest in my nest."
Could it be true? Could it be you?
She hears Him calling! She dreams.
Where are you Lord? She weeps!
In Church! Which Church?
So many church games!
Sitting at the Abbey, her trip,
False smile, crushing grip,
After service, needed a drip
Plastic, stony sunken faces,
Everyone in their right places
Purple circles, gangs, cliques,
Life is better at the Flicks!
Hello! Hi! No eye contact!
Another peck on the cheek!
Bye! BYE! "SEE YOU NEXT WEEK!"
Hurting souls! Need healing!
Weak, weary, worthless and lame.
Searching! Finding church games!
Ran to City Church, just like Ludo
Maybe like colour - coded Cluedo.
Multi colours gowns, multitasks
Red, yellow green and blue,
Straight line, Straight jacket
To join in - roll the money dice.
Treble six, now you are home,

cheesy grins, standing like GNOMES!
Six-digit figures, special red chairs
Sin, what sin? Come on! Come in!
Help her soul! Take her shame,
remove from this shameful disgrace!
How she hates these church games!
Entering a sacred temple like Chess.
Would they honour this simple guest?
Black and white, clean and cool
Quick, remove the fluffy wool
This is regimented and segmented.
King and Queen reign supreme
Bishops, knights, rooks and pawns,
Eloquent, Elegant, Educated, Elevated,
Every heart empty and vacated,
Pumped balloons should be deflated
Her soul longs for righteousness,
Instead she finds political correctness.
Appearing holy, haughty and tame.
A clean set up, just a church game!

BRIDGE

Help! Her soul is burning
Her life needs turning,
Weekly, she is just a number
Tithers are the real members
Her soul seeking for something
hungry, thirsty finds nothing,
Hollow service, another hype
This is just church games!
This Sanctuary is like monopoly
Buying, selling in an Oligopoly,
Bankers keeping all the loot
Men prancing in Italian suits!
Black, pinstripe, bright blue,
Shiny pointed leather shoes,
Bow tie, silk shirts, gold cuff flingsq
Women in purple lace, diamond rings
How much was that thing?
Hunting for filthy lucre,
Instead of men's soul,
Flashy cars, Mansions in Mayfair,
Buy! Buy! Sell! SELL! PROFIT!
Where is salvation for parched souls,
Professional playing church games!
WOW! This is the house of Zion,
No marquees, no masquerade,
Holy Ghost Fire, blazing in the house
consuming impurities, no charades,
Men, women, children and infants,
fasting, praying, singing His praises!
Preacher weeping "Repent! Repent!
On their knees tear stained faces

Looking up to the Saviour for grace,
This is the place! This, is her place.
All sins are forgiven and disgraced
Ultimate reality, not church games!

Give Thanks

When the road of life,
takes that sharp bend,
twisting, turning never-ending
uphill, downhill descending,
can't change gear, accelerating
Screeching! SCREAMING STOP!
Gather your heart! Give thanks!
When the weather turns sour,
prepared for rain, avoiding strain
Suddenly skies turn to black
bombarded with snow and sleet,
jammed in traffic! Twins in the back.
Gutted and flustered! Give thanks!
When it is your turn at ATM,
Keyed in your pin, 50 Euros. No!
Keyed in your pin, 30 Euros. No!
Keyed in your pin, 10 Euros. No!
Quietly tapped Cancel, BROKE!
Two weeks till payday! GIVE THANKS!
Twenty years of devoted love.
Vowed in sickness and health!
My husband, my hero, my turtle dove.
Spell, jinx, hex, out of the blue
Body damaged, savaged, ravaged,
Sucking life, death took advantage.
Widowed in her prime! GIVE THANKS!
Friday, feeling blue, have no clue,
Saturday, clinging the duvet! vexed,
Sunday, hopeless, helpless, worthless
Monday, lethargic, slow, motionless
Tuesday, confused, crushed in spirit,

shut in bottomless dark, deep, damp pit.
Hope dashed! Joy slashed! GIVE THANKS
In high mood or low swing,
In brightness or darkness
Mountain top or deep valley
Abounding or leanness of soul
One thing is required, needful,
Gather your mind, like a Bank
In every situation give.
"In everything give thanks, that is the will of God concerning you in Christ Jesus."

Stolen Childhood

Stolen foetus, forsaking soul,
Sucked, vacuumed like dust,
Product of choice: whistle FOUL!
Dropped in a bucket to decay like rust.
Future gone! GONE! GONE! GONE!
Stolen infant, tiny babes, precious might,
Incubated, helpless, sickened with disease,
Doctors, nurses, carers and parents,
Caring, nursing pain-stricken faces,
No warning: BOMBED! SLAIN!
DEAD IN A RUBBLE! WHO'S GAIN?
Future gone! GONE! GONE! GONE!
Stolen childhood, stolen dreams,
these children, the cream of cream,
in the class, in the gym, lab and hall,
studying Maths, Physics, English, Basketball,
Sprayed with bullets! Shot! Gunned down!
Fathers and mothers working in town.
Future gone! GONE! GONE! GONE!
Stolen teens! Stolen adolescents,
Destroyed dethroning the "age of innocent".
Pornography, fuelling drugs and immorality,
Sponsored by adults around the globe
Uprooting destinies, visions saying no to" Hope".
Teenage mothers, fatherless daily increasing.
Offered welfare, vouchers, mere tokens.
for delicate lives, Jesus redeemed for golden,
Future gone! GONE! GONE! GONE!
Stolen minds! stolen brains,
Dragged from cradle - snatched to drain
Tiny bodies, hunting cobalt in shifty tunnel.

lifting heavy sacks, tiny hands like funnel.
Sifting, inhaling deadly toxic fumes.
These little lambs, sentenced to doom,
for profit: Laptops, iPads, and iPhones all in boom!
Future gone! All gone! GONE! GONE!
Who can restore stolen these years?
There is only ONE that can restore,
There is only ONE that can recall,
There is only ONE that cannot fail;
There is only ONE that cannot change!
"I will restore the years the locusts have eaten!"
Hope in God! Trust in Christ! Faith renewed.
Future restored! RESTORED! RESTORED!

True Freedom at Fifty

NIFTY FIFTY
On the 23rd Jan 1961 the day she was born.
Yes BORN! Now, today 23rd Jan 2011.
This is day, she is supposed to MORN.
The world says now she is filled with SCORN.
She should be filled with anger and TORN!
STOP! EJECT! PRESS! REJECT!
This is the AGE she has been set FREE.
She is FIFTY And NIFTY!
Children are GROWN and GONE
Her Grandchildren are coming ALONG!
No longer the old song
It is TIME for a new TUNE
A new life like HONEY MOON
This the AGE OF CELEBRATION
More time for MEDITATION
NO more MEDICATION
She is NIFTY at FIFTY!
Fantastic! Fabulous! Flattering FIFTY
Gorgeous! Gracious and full of GIGGLES
Filled with a new LIFE! Full of FUN.
Ready to RUN
This RACE has just begun
She is overflowing with LOVE
Like milk bubbling on the STOVE
Yet she feels gentle like DOVE.
Now at FIFTY!
She is HOT like Potatoes!
filled gentleness, tenderness and patience.
loveliness, faith, mercy and grace,
all supplied by His warm embrace.

FROM her lord, The KING OF KINGS!
Now at Fifty
She can LAUGH!
Yes! Laugh at her woes.
No need to worry about her foes.
No longer bound or hounded
by people's opinion
that smells like pungent onions.
At Fifty She is FREE INDEED!
Free to Be who She was made to Be
Free to Explore!
Free to REJOICE!
Free to ROAM or be at Leisure.
She has the assurance of His Love
which He rains down from above.
No longer follows the "JONES"
and constantly posing.
Now she grows her own herbs making poises.
No longer chained by the make-up artist
her wrinkles and crinkles look quite dainty
They are the art work of the MASTER'S hand
Handcrafted and original
made in His Image
Unique, every stand of hair carefully numbered.
Now she can sleep and slumber
No Longer caged like a bird!
She has been set free to fly. Yes FLY!
Till She can reach and touch the sky.
Soaring and gliding high,
balanced and stable.
She now more than able,

She is no longer disabled,
by the words and limitation of men
because she is no longer a pecked hen
It is Nifty to be FIFTY!
She has been set free to do her part
and to do it RIGHT.
No need for figure hugging tights,
She enjoys her life even tough nights.
All her bones and sinews
joins the heavenly choir
to celebrate her liberty
and freedom bought by His Blood
Free from those blue mood.
She is Nifty at Fifty!

She is no longer oppressed,
repressed, depressed, suppressed
No longer nailed to her cross
filled with apprehension followed by more tension.
Her Lord and God has taken he strain,
her anxiety and her pain,
he took away her confusion,
Now she is free from life's delusion.
She raises her head,
Her hands stretched up.
Praise God! Glory to God!
It is Nifty to be Fifty!
She is filled with new HOPE!
No need for that DOPE!
Free to Enjoy her life,
grandmother, mother and wife.

There so much joy, no longer strife,
Yet she eagerly awaits her call,
after her life is spent,
she looks up for heavenly ascent,
to be with her Savior,
and enter the golden gates of splendour
To lay down her head to rest,
because He has prepared her His Nest.
Wow, it is NIFTY to be FIFTY!
The truth is you can be Nifty at Sixty,
seventy, eighty or ninety.
Young people can be nifty at thirteen.
twenty, thirty or forty.
It is not your age or trait
but the ability to CELEBRATE
that Life is worth the living.
So, my friend start singing,
when you cast your cares on Him.
You can be Nifty at Fifty!

God's Kinda Love

God's kinda love is so deep
Yes! Deeper than the deepest pit,
His love is so nice.
It is sweeter than sugar or spice.
God's kinda love is not sleazy,
or hasty, it is not feisty,
You cannot wear it on your sleeve,
because His love cleaves.
God's kinda love,
this love is not rude,
Yes! it is not crude,
It is as gentle as a dove.
God's kinda love
First it gives, and gives
It is so quick to forgive
But best of all it forgets
because God has no regrets!
God's kinda love
is on your mind
when life starts to grind
It never kicks the dust
or make a fuss.
God's kinda love
is like a magnet
draws you close like a dragnet
this love you cannot lose.
You have this kinda love
when you reach out and hug,
instead of holding that grudge,
refusing to wink and nudge.
This kinda love is in your feet
When you say no to mischief,

His love is in our smile
when you go the extra mile.
This kinda love is in your heart
when you turn the other cheek,
even when you are licked and ticked.
God's kinda love
is on your lips
when the words we speak
is kind, gentle and hip,
seasoned with salt
your tongue knows when to halt!
Yes! God's kinda love
is so sweetly neat
like my tartan skirt
clean with pleats.
God´s kinda love works within
When you say no to SIN
that is eating you from within
like jealousy, envy, hatred and lust
just to name a few is a must.
This kinda love can be obtained
From Christ the Lord our Saviour
leaving His splendour, glory, crown
abused treated like a clown.
With love He bore all our sins,
causing him much strain and pain.
On the rugged cross
hung the king of kings
Because of God's kinda love.
Now heaven can be our home
and Jesus pleads with us to "COME!"
This is my kinda love!

The FOOL

The fool utters to himself
"What's the bother there is no God!"
So convince that God is dead.
Logically he argues this in his head.
He goes about not counting the cost,
Unaware of the heavenly host,
that one day he would require his soul.
On that faithful day,
When all accounts are opened,
And all debts must be played.
The fool says in his heart
"Surely there is no fire of hell!"
Then he scoffs "Just a deep dry well!"
Everyone must go to heaven,
his deception rose like yeast in the leaven.
He strokes his palms with glee,
If he dies all this evil he would flee,
So he continues life.
He doesn't suspect the eyes up above,
Like a betrayed husband watching the antics,
of his wife, night after night as,
she roams the towns seducing her lovers,
with her flawless fishnet, frustrated, hooker.
God waits patiently, like a thief in the night,
His judgement will come swift but not out of sight.
The fool says in his mind,
"All I have is mine!"
He grunts "my soul, my wealth!"
All these are mine, even my health!"
So he drinks and makes merry
Sadly he has forgotten, being filled with Sherry,

Every breath belongs to the Master,
The Creator of the universe,
The Alpha and Omega,
The First and the Last.
One day he stands, his mischiefs he must recall!
At the sound of that trumpet call.

Rejoice and be glad: It is only a trial!

My friend, do not relent,
grow cold or weary even in Lent,
Our God is perfect in all His ways.
So, in the time of testing,
please do not go astray.
Let your heart be steadfast,
like a soldier, stand firm, stand upright.
These trials will no last,
don't remove yourself from His sight.
Rejoice and be glad;
it is only a trial!
It will only last a while
Keep praying, fasting,
keep singing and dancing
Fix your eyes on Him and gaze.
Don't be in a haste!
Please, keep a happy face!
Fast if you must,
only remember this truth,
Jesus paid for it all on the CROSS!
Don't lose hope!
Don't go back to the dope!
That is a slippery slope!
You are precious in His Sight
It was for you He fought the gallant fight,
He settled the score,
Once and for all,
signed it in BLOOD with His life!
Refrain from tears,
let go of all that fears.
Rejoice and be GLAD

It is only a trial,
it will be over in a while.
Remember my friend.
the saints of old.
They refuse to grow cold
-Daniel in the lion's cage.
then later he escaped,
-Shadrach, Meshach and Abednego,
even in the hottest flame
they did not grow lame!
OUT OF THE HEAT THEY CAME!
Rejoice and be Glad
This is only a trial.
Please stand and be still!
He will carry you over the hill!
Jesus is Alive! Alive!
Now, you can have a new life.
Beloved, rejoice and be glad!
It is only a TRIAL!
It can only last a while
so you can grin and smile,
you are heaven bound,
because your name,
is in the Lamb's book of LIFE.

Celebrate Jesus, Celebrate

The time has come again,
yes! that wonderful day!
Come snow, sleet, hail or rain,
This is the day that Jesus shines.
It is for this reason we dine.
He came down from Heaven to stay,
bringing peace on earth
goodwill towards men.
Yes! In a stable he was born
among cows, pigs and hens.
In a manger He laid,
His Father and mother had no aid,
in as table forlorn,
the Lord of the earth was born.
Yet! He suffered no depression or ADHD
He grew big and strong
You see to God He belong
filled with the Holy Ghost
power and might,
He had no vice, so he was alright!
A generous soul, his fists were never tight.
When he came to earth,
He knew he would be slain.
yet our Lord he never wain.
Yes Celebrate, Jesus celebrate!
This is the time to let Him shine,
It is because of him we dine,
King Emmanuel came to set us FREE!
Yes! Free from ALL sins,
that drives us from within.
My chains, He broke!

My tormented mind, He stroke!
My wounds, He healed!
My broken heart, He bound
now, I no longer bark like a hound,
or toss to and fro, I can hear a new sound
of his voice saying "I love you! ".
What He did for me
He can do for you.
It is not too late
to be set free,
free from the sins within.
He took my confusion
for which I had no solution
all my problems Christ toss
on the old rugged Calvary cross.
It is time to celebrate!
Come along with me, let us dance,
He has given me a second chance,
it all happened at a moments glance.
when I acknowledge my sins
He covered it with his blood and took me in!
Yes! Let us celebrate Jesus,
it is time for that name to shine.
He is the reason we dine.
Bring out the sweet wine
not fermented, straight from the vine
Roll out the red carpet,
shake off the blanket
Set the festive tables
Our God is more than able!
Christmas has come to stay

Jesus, our lord was born
and later for our sins was slain.
It is time to sing,
Ring the bell ding-a-ling,
The babe in the manger
He is no longer a stranger.
Come on lets us feast!
Come let us eat!
Come one! Come all!
From the north and south,
from the east and west
In Him we can all rest.
Let us join in and feast,
today is the feast of feasts:
turkey and stuffing,
roast potatoes plus a little duckling
glazed ham and seasoned lamb,
baby goose or a fatted calf,
carrots, parsnips, broccoli and sprouts
It looks scrumptious and taste delicious
pasta, noodles, rice and peas,
there is so much choice, eat and be at ease,
curry chicken and goat,
please don't forget the gravy boat!
Ice cream, trifle, apple pie
and mince pies with hot custard
and whipped cream.
This table is a heavenly dream
Apple, oranges, mango juice
white and red grape drink
all fit for the kings of Kings.

Listen, I can hear the heavenly Choir
singing Alleluia, Alleluia! Emanuel!
Yes! Let us celebrate
It was on Christmas morn
That our Saviour was born.
MERRY CHRISTMAS EVERYONE

Mother

The death of a mother
is like no other!
Your heart may skip a beat
when you think of all her treats,
she was so fashionable and neat!
Then your stomach begins to churn
asking to whom do I turn
when life goes wrong,
now she has gone up in glory.
The mind begins to toss
someone is playing a cruel joke.
Stop this not the time to poke
our anger is burning like a flaming CROSS
Quick! Get mother out of that DROSS
Oh Mother! Darling Mother!
Sweet mother! Sweet Mother!
Awake! Awake! Mummy!
Mama! Ma! Mammy!
Don't go! Stay a while
just a little more longer,
a little more time!
This time we vow to be good.
We promise to be true.
Yes! The death of mother
is like no other!
Mummy, I love you!
Mammy, I miss you!
Grand mum, we need you!
Thank-you! Thank-you Mum!
for your toughness full of kindness
for your directness and openness

we honour and salute you!
(Then Wisdom enters the grieving children)
DEATH! Death oh death where is your STING!
Grave where is your Victory!
Christ has risen! Christ has risen!
Through His shed blood
all our sins FORGIVEN!
So we lift up our voices in praise,
because Jesus has gone to prepare
Mummy a better place.
in the Heavens above
filled with joy, peace and Love.
Rest, dearest Mother!
Yes! Rest in Perfect Peace
Adieu! Farewell!
Till we meet again,
In that wonderful land yonder
where there is no more sorrow
Our God controls tomorrow.
Then, together in His sweet embrace
we behold our Saviour's face
full of mercy and grace.
In His presence filled with joy
at His right hand pleasures evermore.
Our Celebrations has just begun,
soon Mother, soon very soon,
we will be together for all eternity.
rejoicing in timeless immortality!
Yes! The death of a mother
is like no other!

Faces!

Faces, faces everywhere!
Yes, faces here and there!
Some black, some white
some dark, some light!
Happy faces, sad faces,
some anxious and depressed by
economic and social recession,
some smiling faces looking like a clown!
I sat, and watched these faces,
Then, I searched for you in that crowd!
I looked and examine with intensity
each and every passing face,
hoping by faith I would see yours,
even just a distant mirage!
Faces there! faces everywhere!
I looked, I searched but yours
was not there, but in my heart
you were there, lurking in every corner
in the shadow, I see you here and there!
Faces, faces all in different frames
but it is for yours I long,
it is for you my heart throngs
to hear your voice singing our song.
Then, I remember,
Now, I recollect,
Now I know I am quite correct,
You are under the earth,
You are six feet beneath,
On top, they laid a holy wreath,
hoping to stop our grief!
Faces, faces, faces,

I looked and searched,
but my son, my dear son,
you were not there!
So I slowed down my pace,
no longer part of this human race!
I can't make haste,
everything is worthless, pointless
an utter, utter waste!
You were my sugar and spice,
all that hot and nice,
Now you are deep down
like Australia you are down under!
Sometimes, I can't go on,
but I know that I've got to carry on!
With Almighty God lifting me up,
the comforting love of the Holy Spirit,
and our loving Saviour Jesus Christ!
I long for the day we will meet again,
in that place so full of grace,
the tears will be wiped from my face.

Don't be a user!

Don't be a user, you will become a loser
Taking advantage of the poor, slaying them at your door.
Peddling drugs, using your thugs - to sell them your dirty rugs!
It is only a matter of time that your mischief,
like a wise thief - will be caught, then locked.
You would be hooked and slammed in the JAM!
This is the judgement of the great I AM!
Don't be a user, you'll end up a loser
Breaking every girl's heart, calling it love,
with your numerous bedfellows, deep in your soul
you know this just a GAME called LUST!
You have become an impregnator,
instead of being a celebrator
of fatherhood, and all things good!
The Father of LIGHT called you to multiply,
husband, wife with godly offsprings.
Then God promised all your needs He shall supply!
and good tidings to you HE will bring.
Please, I urge you don't be a fool,
for if you are a user, you will soon be a loser.
Promising ease taking advantage like a fat cat,
lapping up life's cream milk, lazily slurping it from the mat.
Declaring heaven on earth,
when in truth your counsel is from the pit.
Yes! the pit of hell, deceiving the desperate,
Watch out! Look out! Watch out!
Soon your life will become a hopeless hope,
when you do things that are seedy,

you grab and grab, yet you are parched,
this my friend is GREED
wrapped around your elongated neck.
Let it go! LET IT GO!
This curse will destroy and squeeze every breath,
until you are six feet under
my friend. STOP! STOP!
Don't be a USER or you will be a LOSER.
Instead, I plead emplore you
all who love to use and abuse
open your heart receive by grace
the forgiveness of sin,
let Jesus Christ in.
He will give you a NEW LIFE!
He will take you as His bride a new WIFE.
He will cover you with His Love
He will never leave nor forsake you!
This is the gospel TRUTH
then you can be a WINNER
fresh, new not a loser.

A City in Flames

Here lies a city!
But what a pity!
The smoke is smouldering
coughing and choking
the people are gasping.
This city, my beloved city
Is going up in smoke
Nobody is looking.
It is going up in flames
Women still cooking
so blind, they are not to blame.
I see through the mirror,
A city burnt to ashes.
No-one can remember its name
Hey! What happened here?
A city was there,
Now it is rubble
among the stubble.
A city full of life
Now slain are many wives
5 million in this fine place.
So lofty, Developers, Bankers
Writers, Politicians and Teachers
They all dwelt in this mighty PLACE.
It seems to have fallen from GRACE.
The night life was hustling
Always sucking and bustling.
The people as merry as a lark!
They would always play in the park.
A city so grand!
A people so proud!

What happened here?
In this city aflame.
Prosperity, fame came
Buildings went up and up
Sparkling wine, champagne bubbles.
But now a rotten rubble,
dancing and carousing
like a merry go round.
Fun, giggles, laughter,
in this city so fair.
Let's drink and be merry
Today is the day
Tomorrow is still far.
On the dance floor
On the soapbox
In the pub
In the Hub
FUN! FUN! FUN!
Come on Let's RUN!
The smoke is piping up
Flickering, fanning, choking!
We need to stop carousing
this fair city is dying!
"What is it my love,
What is it my turtle dove?"
A sweet heart whispered
To his beloved
"My body aches
My body in pain
I can't sleep
I can't eat

I toss and turn
This is not fun."
Replied his beloved,
"Come on love
The night is young
Love me again
You are my only dove.
One more pint for the road,
So we can rock and roll"
She croaked like a toad
It is now he must be told.
"My love,
My turtle dove.
The night is young
I cannot go on.
I have something to say,
I can't rock and roll
My body is like a block
The Doctor decree a verdict,
I was hoping it will fade.
I'll be grand! I'll be grand!"
The city is aflame
Burning and smouldering
Carousing and jostling.
Limbs on fire, slowly burning!
Destroying with no warning
I looked in the mirror
Oh, what horror
Our fair city
Engulfed in FLAMES!

Let's Pretend 1

Let's pretend there is no God,
because the world is full of dogs.
Yes! Dogs rule and direct the universe.
They rule, the Earth, Sun, Moon, and Stars.
Let's pretend these dogs evolved,
Yes, in the heat they dissolved,
Then came a chemical reaction,
And brought a new interaction,
Leading to a new direction.
Then everything turned to rubble
Causing all humans to stumble.
Let's pretend, the rain and the sleet
from heavens poured down,
Now, humans all humans can frown.
They saw more chemical reactions,
Then the dust turned into gold,
Then the Sun arose from its' slumber,
Where it did lumber. It shone.
The gold dust glistened,
The humans smiled and gathered
Yes! Gathered the gold dust that scattered.
They laughed and chattered,
from it they made golden images,
A monster, a statute of liberation and named it,
The Stock market - Pure White Solid Gold,
How it glowed! The people rejoiced.
This is a better god than the dogs,

So they danced and worshipped.
This new symbol, stood erect,
so strong, no one could wreck.
"Come and buy and sell,
Please try not to yell!"
Everyone agree, this was beauty to behold,
Beg, steal or borrow, this is it we are told.
A symbol of beauty, health and progress.
Uncertainty gave way to certainty,
Yes! Wealth engulfed recession.
Thus poverty was fought and slain!
The people were no longer in chains.
Behold your god!
Like the Tower of Babel,
The people came paid homage,
This was a great new lineage!
They drank, danced, sang like angels.
It was so hip on this ship!
"Yes! Our God of Gold,
Unto you we must hold,
Now we have no more woes
Gold has defeated our foes."
Then the town went to sleep,
So content they slept deep.
Sown good, it was time to reap!
When they arose late that morning,
The golden statue like Dagon
Had fallen! Yes! Yes FALLEN,
Completely down trodden,
From New York to Tokyo

You can hear the shattering clang,
Our white solid Gold sank!
Toppled from its great height!
Oh! How the stocks had fallen!
Let us pretend, it was a dream.
We must have been in another realm.
Dogs don't evolve and become gold,
Monkeys can't become a man of old,
Man, was made in the image of God.
From dust they came they return to dust.
So what is this evolution fuss!

Made in His image

She arose that morning
Another day!
Another year!
Ouch! She remembers
the tremors of yester years.
It left her in tears.
She strode to the mirror
This day is so distinct,
She didn't dare give a hint
SHE HATED THIS RACE!
It was a disgrace
Look at this face.
Like a woman in the mirror
She examines with groans
The crow feet, the laughter lines,
The wrinkles and ripple dimples
She shrinks and cringes
SHE WAS ADVANCED IN YEARS.
They All smiled back at her – those ugly lines.
She felt like a nutcase,
her life like a shut case
in the darkness of emotions,
she had no notion.
This was commotion
Just like a child,
she examines the surface.
Pop belly, stretch marks,
Hot flushes and more heat
This was not neat
"Menopause stand still!"
She wants to run

Run! RUN to the Sun,
This day was not fun
It has only just begun.
"I want to escape!"
She looks on in her fantasy
She was at ease
She was only 21, dimple cheeks
Ample and supple, like the young Gazelle.
No cares, no fears
Just her and her beloved
Childhood sweetheart
True love endures forever.
The tears streams down her face
It really was too late
Fat, flab, wrinkle lines and more grey hairs
"I am no longer fair!"
I am burnt out, worn out
Exhausted, tired and torn
This menopause is airy
It is very SCARY!
Her tears gushed out like a fountain
Flooding her cheeks
Then she felt his arms,
His strength, as he held her close
His warm tight embrace
She could not resist.
Her beloved arose to rescue her from her FOES
Vanity, self-pity and self-hate - deadly MENOPAUSE
His love is like a drug
Addicted like his masculine hug.
He looked into her eyes

With his lips he kissed her tears
"I love you my darling dove
Dark, shiny and lovely
You are my gift from ABOVE.
Come back to my side
You were taken from my ribs
There you will remain,
You are my soul mate
You're are bed mate
You and I are intimate.
You are mine, 49 years to you,
But you are always 21 years to me.
Love never fades just like JADE
True love endures forever
Till death do us apart.
We will grow old
But our love will grow bold,
With God on our side our love will
Never wax cold.
Come my turtle dove
Remember you were made in His Image
You came from His famous linage
You were fearfully and wonderfully made
Handcrafted and knitted in your mother's womb.
You were one of kind
Now stop looking at your behind,
Come love, come my love,
Back in my arms.
Lay down! There is no harm,
Then, let us snuggle and cuddle
Let us kiss, stop that muddle.
Let us make sweet harmony
To love's perfect symphony.
Her heart melted

His words entered her soul
Like a sword, it pierced her heart
Like a hammer it smashed her doubts.
She looks at him, his eyes captured hers
"I love you my beloved.
Let us go back and savour this moment."
With a glee and shout of pure ecstasy,
SHE SHOUTED AND DECREED!
"Menopause, stand still!"
Love Abound!
Wrinkles and flushes stand on the hill!
Love ride on and ON,
in perfect harmony
to love's true symphony."
"Happy Birthday my turtle Dove!"
He held close.
"Thank you my beloved!"
NB. Rediscover His love ladies.
You are made in His Image,
God loves you. He is your light,
You are precious in His sight.

The Children of tomorrow

Our children, our future.
Our hopes, our song
Come! Let's blow the horn,
Yes my people, there is nothing wrong.
Hip! Hip! Hip! Hooray!
Our children, our tomorrow,
Where there is no more sorrow,
Rise up my Son!
Shine like the Sun!
You see in life,
There is no black or white,
There is no male or female,
No Jew or Greek.
No! There are no GEEKS,
No slaves, we have been set free.
You see my Son,
Your herbs are grown by dews,
That power comes from above
Reach out, Reach High,
Yes, Son reach for the Sky.
Can't you see?
STOP! LOOK! LISTEN!
God is at hand!
Justice is, His Master plan.
Son, let's get real!
This is the real DEAL,
President Obama sits in the Whitehouse,
With his Queen Michelle,
Handsome and beautiful, they excel!
They are the host, with the most
Solid as a rock, hot as Sunday roast,

Clothe with Dignity and intelligent
Working hard they stood the test of time.
Now, they are worth more than a
billion dime
My SON! My TOIL!
You do not know your worth.
Stop drooling and goggling,
Stop fooling, start learning,
You are the child of tomorrow.
For you there is no more sorrow!
Come on Sons!
Get cracking and reading,
Get moving, too much grooving,
You are the children of Tomorrow
No more fears!
No more Tears!
Quit the DRUGS!
Throw out the KNIVES!
Toss the GUNS!
Be Sober! No more slumber!
Come on, get rid of those CANS!
Be drunk in this new wine
It is free of charge,
It is ELECTRIFYING!
It comes from ABOVE,
Not MORTIFYING!
With this SPIRIT you can get high,
Get Holy power like dynamite.
Sons, quit messing,
Start investing,
Get my drift

Or do you still need a lift?
God is in the land!
Discrimination has no mouth!
Get out the tambourine!
Lets the school bell RING!
Let's make aloud
DING-A-LING-LING!
Like Martin Luther-King's dream
Son, you are the CREAM.
Yes! You are the child of tomorrow,
For you there is no sorrow.
My Sons, don't go astray!
Don't just stare and GAZE!
Quick Sons and make haste,
Opportunity knocks,
Here's the key now the lock,
The doors are open wide!
Talents and gifts are in,
Don't bury them, one, five or ten.
Start using them, don't be a hen!
Grab your books, Study! STUDY!
Start serving, get leading!
Keep praying, no quitting!
Son, you are one of a KIND
Fearfully and wonderfully made,
Unique in every way,
You are the child of TOMORROW
For you there is no SORROW.

53

At 53
I am like an Oak tree!
Planted by the riverside of life.
Watered by His awesome tide,
By Grace, I have nothing to hide.
Bringing forth seasonal fruits
Declaring everywhere the
Fragrant of God's LOVE & TRUTHS!

Mothers to Daughter — Marriage Secrets

Hello Daughter!
Life is full of laughter.
Now that you are married.
Draw closer and ponder
gain wisdom from yonder.
Keep your ears open,
take a deep breath then glean
because you are no longer a teen!
A man has many needs,
as a wise woman take heed,
your husband has chosen you my dear,
above beautiful gazelles and deers.
When he looked for a wife
in you he found his better half.
Mum! Mum you ask
What is my new task?"
With your eyes open wide
marriage is like a roller-coaster ride
All that education gave you no clue
What a real woman should know
When she says "I do!"
You're chosen my daughter
to love him like no other.
I am from the old school
Modern women must stand still.
Marriage is like a steep hill,
Life is not about being cool
they need to have the right tool.
Now that you two are one,
listen, look and learn.
Don't be in a hurry,

slow down and tarry.
Be gentle and mild.
In God's image you are made
To be your lover's Help-Mate!
Your part my daughter
Is to love him like no other,
"The best way to man's heart
Is to feed him well, then massage
every ego to make his burden light
you will bring him pure delight!
When he comes home uptight,
He has been working 9 till night,
His stomach starts to growl,
In a loud voice, he howls.
Please be swift and quick
Get his meal on the plate
Three meat, two veg and gravy to lick
You see he needs Cook-Mate!
When he looks worn and torn,
His comments full of scorn,
From the gym, he sweats with the heat.
Please don't use your words to beat,
Fill the tub with warm soapy water
make him a soothing altar.
then gently scrub, him with a loofah
Your man needs a Bath-mate!
When he turns the lights low
And he is burning from below,
My dearest child, keep your tongue,
Dive into Lingerie, fishnet tights,
with a dash of cologne,

it is going to be such a night
Straighten your hair, flash him your best smile,
Your man is ready for a Bed-mate!
When his pulse is running high,
His temp soar more than 39,
In his eyes you see the tears.
They are darkened, full of fears
Sneezing, puffing coughing,
Spluttering and muttering.
Don't watch him in PAIN!
Take off his strain.
It is time to be his Nurse-Mate!
When he feels a wreck,
Losing that contract and job,
He thinks he's a jerk!
He has lost all the perks.
He is sinking, no longer thinking,
Girl, take the hold of the paddle,
Stir the ship of your marriage,
This is not time for carnage
He needs you to be his Ship-mate!
When he is feeling down,
He has bought into that lie,
That imprisons the mind,
Depression is looming,
Suicide thoughts, so gloomy
Resist your tongue, don't hammer
Get on your knees like Hannah!
Call on Father, Son and Holy Ghost
What he need is Prayer- Mate!
When the budget is low,
And the account is bright red.
Darling, don't be misled,
Step up boldly, sell a few of your attires,

Be sure to keep the one he admires
In the secret, balance the books,
But please don't be a crook.
Right now, you are his Bank-Mate!
When you see him carrying
Every child, nieces and nephews
Babies in his arms and not a few
He's eager to feed them with stew
Pay attention, men can brood
They are not a prude.
Take heed, don't delay
This can be rude.
Don't argue or be crude
He wants you to be a Mother-mate!
When it is all said a done,
marriage is the best institution
without any hesitation
with its' trials and tribulations,
there will be strive and doubts,
Please don't opt out!
Remember who design the marriage
He knows the two in your carriage,
Always pray for wisdom form above
And be as gentle as a dove.

The Child in me

There is a child in me
that wants to get out,
that wants to shout,
"I believe in the Father
The Son and the Holy Ghost"
and knows this is not a hoax.
Inside me there is a child,
playing Jekyll and Hyde,
striving to climb to bale out,
convinced that the impossible
is naturally possible
by the great I AM that I AM!
Yes! Inside of me there is a child
that trusts and believes,
in that mighty name Jesus.
The Blind can see!
The lame can walk!
The dumb can speak!
The dead will rise!
The child knows this not a game
Jesus brings no shame.
In my soul there is a child,
contending yet sweet and mild,
wanting to cry, wail and lament,
"I have sinned, am filthy like a rag,
looking and feeling like a hag,
I need to be clean from within
who can deliver me from a life of SIN!"
Inside me this child,
gentle, kind but strong,
acknowledges I am wrong

and points me to the cross
asking me to lay down my woes,
receive pardon, freedom from foes.
That child in me,
wants me to be set free,
by the shed Blood on Calvary.
All I need to is to reach out,
All I need is to speak out!
Admit, believe then confess,
Then receive grace, no FUSS.
There is a child in me
that knows the truth,
But the Adult inside
full of fear and cares
embraces the lies
with a soothing smile.
rejects, retract and refrains
until the child in me slowly dies!
Is there a child speaking to your heart to step out in
faith today?
"Remember without Faith it is impossible to please God."

31

Keep Strong!

When you need a helping hand,
but you find trouble in your land.
When the wicked appear to flourish,
your soul is parched,
No dosh, no nosh!
My friend, keep strong.
Hold on tight,
Tackle that fright,
Let Jesus in your heart,
It is going to be alright!
Keep strong just hold on.
When friends betray,
and family ties are in disarray,
neighbours your friendship reject,
only your faults they detect,
stand firm, meditate and reflect.
Keep strong! Hold on!
Jesus is coming,
He won't be long,
Keep going! Yes! Keep strong!
When your body is invested with sores,
Wailing, crying, screaming, shouting,
"This must be a curse!"
When you go for diagnosis
and receive fatal prognosis,
Remember this, hold on!
By His Stripes you are healed,
with His Spirit you are filled,
Keep Strong! Go on!
It won't be long, Keep Strong!
When you are heavy laden,

know you are not in heaven.
Stress weighs you down,
life treats you like a clown.
Another death, another loss,
these hurts sucks, what a dross,
Shouldn't life be like Candy Floss?
Hold on! Keep strong!
Come to the Cross,
all your problems toss!
Hold on, Keep strong!
When fierce storms are raging,
Violent gales roaring, destroying,
defying, so daring not caring.
Stand firm! Stand up! Stand Strong!
Strengthen those weak knees,
Resist! Resist evil and it will FLEE!
Hold on! Keep strong!
"Life is a long journey!"
Don't take the wrong turning!
Hold tight! Fight the good fight!
Hold on! Keep Strong!

Adieu

"Farewell, Adieu"
On the sixth of May
What a fateful day!
my husband of 30 years
handsome and fair of face,
was granted God's grace,
When he declared "no more pain ",
he was on cloud seven.
his spirit ascended to heaven
returns back to the father above
precious servant, angels with a new song,
with cymbals, harp and a gong
shouting Alleluia, Alleluia!
The Lord God Omnipotent reigns!
Adieu my beloved
farewell my darling
Rest in perfect Peace!

Let's pretend 2 - Death and Grief!

Let's pretend
life moves on
even though this loved one has gone!
Let's continue to eat, drink and be merry.
"We are sorry mate, hard luck mate
for him it was too late!
We'll say a couple of "Hail Mary's".
Let's pretend
He never existed!
Then we can be what we want to be.
Let's say nothing, do nothing.
Even though his face we see everywhere,
on the buses, streets, shops and church.
"Look again, can't you see him,
eating, sleeping, laughing and singing,
his presence is in our midst lingering."
Let's pretend,
He never died!
He never lived!
In our mind he was never born,
so we can ease our pain,
and remove this evil chain.
Let's pretend
this life never ends!
He has gone to heaven,
just like number seven!
"My friend, please get real.
this is the real deal,
His life was torn asunder.
Come on! He is six feet under!"
Let's pretend

his parents had three not four,
we stop counting the score,
quickly block out his handsome face,
let our mind block out his name,
then everything can remain the same.
"Hold on mate, isn't this childish
to play these mind games?"
How long can we pretend?
Oh! How low we did descend.
Was he not made in God's image?
Until death came and slain!
Let us work through this,
Weeping and wailing,
Christ's love demonstrating,
reaching out with mercy
be the good Samaritan,
ending this pretense marathon!

Rescued

Wearing her purple gown,
so sophisticated but sultry,
off to the streets she goes,
searching from head to toe.
Like a jaded old clown,
she is looking for love,
hunting for her turtle dove!
Day and night her aching heart
cries out to anyone and everyone.
Someone to break her fall,
when she slips,
like a banana split.
Her virtues have been
stolen, tossed to and fro,
like an open door,
she has been used,
and abused.
Now she walks the shopping malls,
sometimes she waltzes, dancing
in the night clubs,
looking for hugs,
heavily made up,
thick black liner,
to cover the shame
of that big shiner,
received unexpectedly,
when she thought
she had found him!
Now she knows that
"Lust" is a deadly game.
Sometimes she goes bare,

No make-up, lipstick
mascara or eye shadow
no more hiding her sorrow.
Her face says it all,
"Love me if you please,
This is who I am, please do not tease!"
Then she would look into her mirror,
all she could see was a hall of horror,
lines of stress and loneliness,
in a state of hopelessness,
surrounded her helplessness,
seeking and hunting for love,
drunk in her desperate desire.
So broken and worn,
her life she lays bare,
she was in a mess,
in mental distress
her inner soul ripped and torn.
Then she cried, wept,
"like a bruised reed,"
hanging on a thread,
she wanted to be freed,
she sought for a friend,
to hear her woes,
but the people she knew
became her foes,
she was a loser,
nobody wanted to know.
Her head sank low,
her feet were slipping,
her steps were sliding,

"Who could rescue me,
from these besetting sins,
that lies deep within?"
For a split second
her world stood still,
an invisible hand, reached out
like the bells of St. Clements,
she heard that audible voice,
"it was for you I came,
to take away your shame."
She looked up above
tear stained, she grabbed His hand,
He pulled her out of her Miry Clay
where The ENEMY would have her stay.
When she looked at Him,
His fire flamed eyes pierced
through the core of her soul,
He would not let her go,
He was like a magnet
glued to this starlet.
Through her tears, she marveled,
His body was so riddled and marred,
"Is that you Lord," she asked.
"Why are You so bruised?"
His blood trickled into her hand,
each drop cleansing, as it lands
"I did it all for you my daughter,
to forgive and deliver you,
to fill you with joy and laughter."

A NEW REPUBLIC

Hey Dude! What's the story?
Do you want to be cool?
Then listen friend and don't be a fool,
Something good is about to happen,
Something good, no-one can dampen,
Can't you see, the laws are changing?
A new dawn is rising,
The old republic has fallen,
Sit up my friend!
Don't be the new fiend,
Take heed and do good
This is the new rule
Don't be a mule,
Old things have passed away,
New things are on the way.
Yes, evil is out of date,
Love of money must be slain,
Greed and gluttony must be dumped,
Slander and gossip must not be pumped.
Malice, murder and violence have been tossed
along with wickedness, that filthy dross.
If you want to stay
It is our Goliath we must slay.
Goodness, kindness, and mercy find,
Gentleness, caring and sharing,
from these do not hide.
Hey dude, stay cool,
You don't need the pool,
Love in hate is sin
It is sane, to reach out and touch,
That's not too much,

Drunkenness, lewdness and carousing,
Looting, fighting and cursing
All these comes from within,
It is time to purge these things.
In this new republic,
there is a purity boom,
For wickedness there is no room,
Unless we want to be doomed.
You see friend,
It is a new day,
Let's make hay
There is no more depression,
There is no more repression,
We have no more oppression,
No more delusion,
so we have no more recession.
Drugs out,
Let's all give it some CLOUT.
Let's boot it OUT
And give a SHOUT!
No more money laundering,
We must work hard for a living,
Come on dude!
Can't you conclude?
It is the New Republic
It is a new and living way,
Everyone has a say
We are not dismayed.
It is a new morn
Today many are born
Come on lets' blow the horn.

We'll make a toast,
To the new political host
This new republic
Will be full of grace
And like Wilberforce,
Will set people free.
Black, White, Greek or Jew,
Now we are in a pasture new,
We can eat together in the same stew.
Come on brother! Come on sister!
Let LOVE take the strain
The milk of human kindness,
Spreading its multicultural branches,
So we can experience tenderness.
This is the new way to be cool
Stop that messing, don't be a fool
Truth, love and morality
This is the new reality.
It is a new day!
It is a new dawn!
Yes, a new morn!
Welcome Queen and Obama!
Good bye NAMA!
A new republic, full of grace
Now we can walk the streets
And show our face
Come to Ireland
And taste,
Be quick and make haste
It is Fine Gael, in a new coalition,
There will be new solutions,

Let us pray, there will be
No more confusion.
This is the new REVOLUTION
It is so grand! Yes, really GRAND!
This is our kind of EVOLUTION!

The best is yet to come

As I remember you face
The warmth of your grace,
When you choose me
To be your beloved wife,
You gave me a new life.
It was your smile
Straight, white
Dazzling all neatly lined
Each one in place.
I remember your timing,
It was 7.30pm
It was our special date.
You were never late,
You were on time at my gate.
I remember your mind
You were one of a kind
Always calm
You had so much charm.
I had to have this man
Or I will be damned.
I remember it all seems so wrong
Were we in love or just in lust?
You were my song
It was for you my heart did throng
You were everything to me
You were all I need.
You made me feel so neat
Even in the heat.
That was then
Now 31 years on
5 pregnancies gone,

4 children born
All my work is nearly done.
If I had to choose
I would not loose
Time and be a goose,
I will gladly step on the altar
I will take again that tall order.
In sickness and in health
Till death do us apart
Till Jesus come
To take us home.
I will say it boldly
I will say it loudly
You are the one for me,
My true love.
Let me be your turtle dove
From now and forever more.
May your latter days
Be better than your former years.
May God help to defeat your fears.
May you be the head and not the tail.
May your foes run and wail.
May you see your children's children.
May you find the love of your brethren
May your children possess the gates of
your enemies.
May God restore the years that the
locust has eaten
May you never be beaten.
May your wife be a fruitful vine.
May your house be filled with new wine

May the Lord God bless and establish
The works of your hand,
May you possess the land.
May He grant you your heart's desire.
and set your hand on fire.
As you delight yourself in Him
May your sight never grow dim.
May the Lord bless and keep you,
Cause His face to shine upon you
And keep you in all your ways.
For the rest of your days
May God bless you
Happy birthday Darling.

Shepherd Oh Shepherd

"Shepherd of my people
answer me please!"
Can you sit,
where My little one's sit?
Can you digest and eat
what they were forced swallow
when they lay in sorrow?
Will you feed them
with pastures green
so their lives remain clean?
Can you drink
what My children drink?
When afflicted in trouble
deep in Miry Clay.
Will you reach out
when they tumble?
Can you live,
where My people live?
In a tiny rundown flat
so small no room for a hat!
Then you demand more rent
for your home, like a fat cat!
Can you give
as My poor give?
With a sacrifice of praise,
their widow's mite
yet so full of FAITH,
willing to praise,
bringing honour to my gate!
Can you, Pastor,
shepherd My flock
you call "my lot"?
Remember they are sheep,

sometimes they sleep,
but their soul, you must keep.
when in despair they weep.
Can you Preacher,
now big and strong,
remain a humble teacher,
caring and tending them when wrong?
Can you help them,
strengthen them,
instead of pollute
and delude them?
Can you, Vicar,
remove your rolled cigar,
and the caviar
to lay down your life
and forget the Hype?
Honour My call
to love the weak,
even when they reek!
Mighty man of God,
As my anointing upon you fall.
Please bless do not curse
strolling down that magnificent hall
chest puffed up ten feet tall.
In your own eyes, remain small.
Shepherd oh my shepherd,
Bless My people
Love all My children'
Nurse My little lambs
"Feed My sheep"
I neither slumber nor sleep
I AM is watching you,
in all you do!

It must be great!

It must be great to be white,
when everybody thinks you are always right,
and you seem to be the only one in the light.
What a pity to be black
from conception you suffer rejection,
from birth you are defeated
everyone thinks you come from beneath,
you always seem to lack because you are dark.
However, it is much greater to be a child of God,
because against the odds,
Black or white you are in his mighty hand
routed and grounded in Him (CHRIST)
You are the apple of is eye,
So in Him you have the true LIGHT.
It must be great to be white,
when your words are believed
until the truth is revealed,
always innocent before guilty.
How sad to be black.
when your words are decoded
and said to be a hype and loaded
always guilty until proved innocent.
It is much greater to be washed by His blood,
Guilt of sins that lies deep within,
Able to bow your head and say
"Forgive me LORD, I am a sinner,
I need your grace."
And without haste
You receive his pardon.
Set free and not abandoned.
It must be great to be a white woman

Blond, brown, brunette, blue, green-eyed
she is labelled a role model,
the epitome of womanhood,
with rosy skin so soft and silky
like peach so milky.
A beauty to be hold,
the desire of every manhood.
What a disgrace to be a black woman,
At a glance crowded and branded,
an ugly witch and a bitch,
she is just here to get rich,
home wrecker, a harlot,
another bump, another lump,
all her children on the welfare she dumps
in a damp refuge this is her lot.
How wonderful to be a woman that fears the Lord,
this woman God will not scold,
her worth, more costly than GOLD.
She has been bought by the His BLOOD
washed and made whole no longer a slave
She has now become a SAINT.
Her price is far above rubies because
she is cherished and beloved by her Master
as she surrenders her life at His Altar.
This woman shall be praised.
It must be great to be a white child
hardly scolded or given a good spank,
because the effect could turn their mind blank,
handsome, charming, smart and intelligent,
potential lawyer, director, doctor or a banker.
These are our future so we must invest,

and help to support the family nest
so let them eat, play and rest.
How tragic to be a black child,
malnutrition, feeble mindless and a ridicule,
dump, dull, full of deceit, you see they "have no clue.
Accursed be ragged, wanderer and a vagabond,
rioters, thieves because they are society rejects,
for the sake of peace we must neglect
and from our community eject!
They can't read, hardly write,
what they need is a good hide!"
It is much greater to be the child of the Living God,
Forgiven, filled with grace and mercy,
He is surrounded by God's love
and he is favoured from above,
like "Timothy" he has seen the Light.
This child of God will always shine bright
like the stars he will be Alright.
Remember that God created mankind in His image.
There is neither male or female, Greek nor Jew, all were
made in His sight.
Be true and just treat others the way God treats you. He
made the sun to shine on the just
AND the unjust. To all that comes to him he turns
none away. He warns us to be kind to the
foreigners and treat them with justice.
He is looking down and we each have to give an account
to Him. He sees all things even in the
dark if it is light.
Let us remember to love.
Where there is love there is God.
where there is no love there is not God.
God is LOVE!

Gotta fake it to make it

Another day!
I feel like a lump of clay,
it is the same routine
I need to get myself a new tune.
Oops! gotta get to the bathroom
I feel so gloom
I need to groom.
Looking at myself
In the mirror
Oh, golly gosh what horror!
My nose dips and spreads out flat,
like the back of a bat.
My lips are so big and thick
like McDonalds milkshake
so sweet to lick.
My eagle eyes are big and round
Dark Brown like the dirt the on ground.
My skin smooth, dark and tanned
yet I still feel banned
I feel like Jane - so plain!
Oh, what a pain.
I look at my behind
Yelp! I need to hide!
All that potato chips
seems to settle on my hips
Wow! look at my dip,
it matches my lips.
I look at the top
I see my curly bop
all curly and crinkled
like my little wrinkles.

I feel so sad,
I think I've been had,
I need some changes
or I'll go crazy!
Just look at this shape,
look at this face,
It is a disgrace
Help! I need some grace.
Then I remember Mama said
and on her words I fed.
"Gal don't screw up your face!"
Put on your best lace
a dash of cologne
Don't be home alone.
Put on a big smile,
The world will only hold you for a while.
If you want to make it
You've gotta fake it!
I look again at my mirror
I tried a smile,
The gal smiled back.
I can hear Mama
'Gal don't be slack
take some cash,
Put on some dash
You've gotta fake it to make it.!
I look on my wall
Their suit hangs tall
It's my slimlined silhouette.
No diet! No fuss

No pills! please hush
This cloth is a must
if you have to go burst.
If you want to make
You've must fake it.
I slipped it on
this is my all-in-one body illusion,
it is my final delusion
which adds to the confusion.
Men, please don't get mad
and say you've been had
You've gotta agree
In it I look like a PEDIGREE.
Here's looking at you Gal!
Yes! I say it with pride,
I have nothing to hide
Now, I can wear a lofty smile,
Instantly, I am in dream
Flatter tummy,
Hmm I look yummy!
Yes, quite scrummy.
Slimmer thighs
now I am feeling high,
firmer buttock.
I can wear that new FROCK.
No more shocks
With my new uplifted burst
now you agree that is a must.
This maybe an illusion
but I feel sensational
Thanks Mama!

I've gotta fake it to make it!
My people get to grips
and don't be such a drip.
I need to fake it to make it!
I need to make it to the top,
I don't want to be flop,
all this is a must
even if my account goes burst!
The make-up – the nail
I look at my toe nail
Now, I start to wail.
Dry, chapped n' bitten
I'm quite smitten
I need my Nailwear Pro,
for the gal that's on the go
You see this kinda mess
must be hidden.
Quick brush and blow,
With my nail protect diamond dust,
I have product promise, it will not rust!
Wow! A swipe and a wipe
I know it all a hype!
Can't you see?
With these new colours,
I am looking cool,
Now I feel great,
What a taste!
With this polish
There is no waste,
Yeah Mama!
Ride on mama
I need fake it to make it!
The make-up – The face
I took my brush,

now I am in a rush,
I gotta getta work.
Put on some eyeliner.
Wow that opened my eyes!
Took my mascara
that lengthened my lash
Mmm! It looks real dash
good work for the cash.
I took a damp sponge
retoned my skin.
Now I am looking sleek
with my new ebony glow
I ran my finger down my cheeks.
That's my kinda flow!
I am looking good,
I am feeling bold,
Now I'm not cold.
Agree Mama!
I've gotta fake it
just to make it!
I took my lipstick
Wild berry with honey plum,
it tastes great just like gum
this stick is my chum!
I am looking good
I am feeling great
Great Mama
I've gotta fake it to make it!
I look at my curly bop
it needs to be straight
if I want to get to the top
you see I need a plait,
quick I won't be late!
I hooked on my wig.

Pow wee it looks so gig!
This is my new hair piece
now I've got peace!
Looking like Tina Turner!
Now watch, those heads
turn at the corner!
Kudos to you Sasha!
Looking good gal!
Feeling cool.
Whoops something is missing
What is it girl?
I need a special catch
or this image will have a patch.
I reached out for my Prada
It cost little more cash
And it smells better than hash
Good on you Mama!
Now I've fake it, hope I make it!
A new face
With my new lace
Everything is in place
I need some grace!
I gave a smile
That's the extra mile
Here's the world's image
Now Sasha take the stage
You've gotta fake it to make it!
I gave another smile
I stepped outside
Now for my free ride
I am looking like Dynamite
I feel like toast on Marmite.
Stood at the bus stop
Gotta make it to the top

Cars speeding by,
slowing down
whistling, staring and glaring
I feel like a clown.
I flash my smile
they stop and cooed.
"Hey babe looking good
Want a lift?
It is my gift!"
I chuckled and giggled
Mama was right.
You gotta fake it to make it!
I got on the bus,
I got a free ride.
Every man gave me the eye
every wife gave me a sigh
I gotta fake it to make it!
Gotta work! Gotta work!
Oops I missed the deadline
My Boss, Mr B, smiles,
Wink, wink, it is all in his blink.
"Sorry Mike, I couldn't complete!"
"No worries you and I have a date
I'll tell the wife I will be late,
That's my gal!" he chimes!
Then, he slurps and burps.
Now I am scared Mike is a flirt
I feel cheap like dirt!
Help me I am not Tina Turner
This is quite a horror!
I want to do a runner.
Closed his door,
I sat at my desk
Oh what the heck!

Remembering Mama
"You've gotta fake it to make it."
In the middle of the day
the heat took control
I must get out and stroll
I began to sweat
My waxed face begins to melt
and gives odious smell!
Quick back to the loo
before I become a fool.
I need a touch up, brush up!
Phew! Much better all the heat.
Stress, torn and worn
I have taken another beat.
Few minutes, back on my seat
I began to perspire
My body is stuck in this wire
I am out of date - EXPIRE!
My new human wig.
no longer silk like a string,
When will it all end?
Back and forth
In then out of the loo
this washroom is my igloo.
It is cold like ice
I try to feel nice.
Now I know I am the FOOL!
Instead I feel like a joke
then something spoke
in my heart a sweet song
'Jesus loves me this I know
for the Bible tells me so'
little ones to Him belong
they are weak but He is strong!"

That's the voice of Miss Poole
From my old Sunday School
In this world of plenty
Why am I still feeling so empty?
This is not me, It is a mirage
Staring in the Mirror! Whose Image?
Trying to become a rake,
I have become so Fake!
I am a human disgrace!
I feel like a sad case!
The tears began to flow
Now where is my ebony glow?
Knowing I have been a fool
Dashed back to the loo.
in there it is COOL!
I stripped my wig,
revealing tiny curly rings
Removed the mascara,
Cleansed my eyeliner
I look at my deep brown eyes
They look rather nice.
I walk back to my office
nobody took notice
I sat on my desk
"Oh what the heck!
I won't fake it to make it!"
My boss comes out
He took a stumble,
then he shouts,
'I like the hair do,
it is really you!'
My mates were amazed
They just gazed
'Who's the new girl'

'I like her skin tone'
I smiled and agreed
'Thanks guys!
I am done with the wig
No more tones!
No more groans!
No more delusions
to get my solutions."
"Take me or leave me
Yes! I look like Jane,
with no strain, just plain!
I have no more pain.
In my heart, I have recovered,
now that I've discoveredI am made
in His Image
And He is so full of grace."
I closed my file
Ready for that extra mile
This time I can smile
I won't fake it to make it!
Nobody whistled!
No glaring or staring!
No free rides from stalkers!
gone were the curb crawlers.
Simply me, the real me!
Completely and utterly free,
so neat, inside I feel clean!
No Mama! I am ME!
I won't fake it, to make it!
Jesus loves me!
This fact, I now know.
Now my inside glows
from the Holy Ghost's blow!
No longer need my hair piece

because I have the Prince of Peace.
I can't fake it to make it!
Dedicated to all my black sisters
trying to make it in this world.
You are bought with the precious
blood of Jesus.
You are Unique, one of a kind!
You are made in His Image!
He loves you! He will never
leave you!
Call on Jesus and He is so close.

Song of Surrender!

(Please sing to the tune "Kumbaya my Lord")
Have your way Lord,
Have your Way!
Have your Way Lord!
Have your Way!
Have your Way Lord,
Have your Way!
Oh Lord have your Way!
Come on in Lord,
Come on in!
In my heart Lord,
Come on in!
Come in Lord
Come right in!
Oh Lord have your Way!
Chorus
Have your Way Lord!
Have your Way! ×3
Oh Lord have your Way!
Not my Will Lord,
But your Will!
Not my Will Lord
But your Will!
Oh Lord have your Will!
Have your Way Lord
Have your Way ×3
Oh Lord Have your Way!
Enter in Lord!
Enter in!
In my heart Lord,
Enter in!

Enter in Lord,
Enter in!
Oh Lord have your Way!
I surrender ALL!
Come on in!
I surrender ALL!
Come on in!
I surrender Lord
Come on in!
Oh Lord have your Way!
Chorus
Have your Way Lord!
Have your Way× 3
Oh Lord have your Way!

Only 24 Hours

You have only 24 hours!
Time bows, salutes you
then rises, beckons you
next mentally cajoles you!
You have only 24 hours!
Don't belittle or devour!
Don't hate or turn sour!
Don't be grudge another.
You have only 24hours!
Now forgive and forget.
Now make that final call!
Now let love honour all!
You have 24 hours!
No time to murmur!
No time for rumour!
No time for a detour!
You have 24 hours!
Be wise! Be giving!
Be gentle! Be loving!
Be a good neighbour!
You only have 24 hours
Times up! All hopes gone!
Empty bed! Shattered dreams!
Inside a box no longer cream.
You have only 24 hours!
Death comes to devour!
Last breath but a vapour!
Here is Judgement the Saviour!
The Widow in our midst!
There is she again,
in our midst
always in red,
As if she is never fed!

Here she is again
In our midst,
She sticks out
like a traffic light,
refusing to change from red!
Why can't she stay in bed!
Here she goes again,
Stuck in our midst!
Smiling and cooing,
Like an old hen,
Her feathers are bright red,
Who let her out the pen?!
Here she is again,
sitting in our midst.
Doesn't she have a place to go!
Daily, she's covered in red,
where is she from, nobody knows!
She is here again
In our midst!
Standing! Clapping!
Why is she so happy!
Draped in that coat - Blood Red.
With all her woes and troubles,
She should have fled!
Here she is again
in our midst!
Jumping and singing!
Swaying and dancing
with many other women
All dressed in pure, shocking red.
Extremely happy and joyful despite,
all the tears they gave shed!
Here they are again

in our midst!
Now I know who they are!
These are the Lord's widows!
Like me, their sins are forgiven,
Cleansed and washed by His Blood,
The blood of the lamb of God!
They are set free! Yes! Free indeed!
To worship and adore their Saviour!
In His eyes, all widows find favour!
Here they are again
in our midst!
Our eyes have shunned them!
Our mouths have taunted them!
Our hearts have rejected them!
But you oh Lord loved them!
Forgive us, Forgive Lord!
Give us another chance!
Give us a new heart!
So we can take a second glance
with your love abiding in us,
we promise to
reach out to all,
even when they fall!
Have prayed for a widow today?
Have you phoned or text a widow today?
Have you visited a widow today?
Widows are precious to God!
Are they precious to you?
Why not adopt a widow and show her
The Love of God!
This is true religion!

Fools get wise

A simple fool gushes, acting cool,
treating his enemies and foe.
as friends of old, holding them close
until they hack him like a hen,
nailing bare bones to his pen.
My oh my, what a simple fool!
A double fool so easy to enchant,
uttering falsehood, flatteries and lies.
They lead him to their chambers,
hungry to be the "in the crowd!"
Smiling, snorting and sniggering,
they escort him to his slaughter
screaming, stuttering till he dies.
My oh my, a double fool!
The biggest and saddest fool
puffs up his chest, floating in pride
despises his ordained helpers.
Feeds them with scorn and hate,
refuse to take their helping hands!
Sinking low,whoops it is too late!
He curses them with his mouth!
Chases them with his feet!
Loathes them in his heart!
Then cries to God to send help.
My oh my, what a BIG Fool!
The wise fool comes to his senses
He remembers his father's warning
seeing the fangs behind the smile,
the claws underneath the nails,
whiskers covering the thin lips.
The mask reveals the evil within!

His mother's law in mind.
He turns, makes haste and runs!
"This is the way - walk ye in it!"
My oh my, this fool got wise!

How can I forget?

How can I forget?
A child fair of face
eloquent, full of grace
born to join this rat race.
Yet, he was never a disgrace!
How can I forget?
This youth who grew in faith.
6′2″ tall, strong, solid in stature.
At 18 never had a first date
In his heart he grew no hate.
Loving kindness was his game.
How can I forget?
My son, whom I nursed
from my breast he fed,
weaned from milk to bread,
Full of fun and laughter.
Suddenly led to the slaughter!
How can I forget?
This child innocent and fair.
A health body and mind
At 17 years riddled with CANCER!
Lumps, clumps and bumps
Like and old man of seventy
Yet! No one had the answer!
How can I forget?
His tiny racing cars,
laid orderly across the hall.
Trailed up the stairs to the kitchen.
Quick to design, complex structures
that only God could nurture.
How can I forget?

His basket ball hoop,
standing erect in the garden.
Morning by morning he rose
by dawn, running, jumping!
Thud, thud, dribbling the ball!
Then leaping like a kangaroo
Ready, steady DUNK!
Yeah! It's in the net. My hero!
If he missed his face sunk.
Like a divine call, he never quits!
He try again, again and again!
How can I forget?
The news! The diagnoses!
Hospital visits and prognosis!
Watching him go bald.
Mannerly, he remained bold
Week after week he kept
his faith and refuse to faint!
Despite treatment never grew cold!
How can I forget?
My babe, my boy, my son!
Now a man, refused to complain
"My Cross Mum! My Cross!"
He whispered in my ears,
this Chemo I vow to toss .
How can I forget?
They can forget!
They have no regrets!
To the hospital he is a number!
To the family just a member!
To the church he's gone to heaven!

To me this was living in hell,
and no one to tell!
How can I forget ?
The child from my womb
How can I forget the years!
How can I forget the tears!
How can I stop the fears!
Now my man child lay in the coffin,
in beige suit bloated like stuffing!
Then I heard a whisper!
"They can and will forget!
Even Mothers can forget!
I Am the I Am will never forget!
Open your eyes and see!
His name is inscribed in my palm!
He is safe with me the Hope of glory!
This is the truth it is not a story!

Give me chance - A foetus plea!

Give me a chance!
Mother Dear Mother!
Give me a second glance
I will make you proud!
Give me a chance!
Let me join the human race,
putting a smile on your face
I would make you laugh!
Give me a chance!
Promise not to cry!
When you want to sleep
Really Mama, I'll try!
Give me chance!
I'll work very, very hard!
Cram my 1,2,3 and A,B,C,
I'll be first, you'll see!
Give me a chance!
I won't be a bore!
I'll do my chores,
Mom! I will be clean!
Give me a chance!
To become the Cream,
Celebrate my dreams
Mum, GIVE ME LIFE!
Give me chance
to dance my dance,
to sing my song,
Celebrate each day!
Give me a chance
to be like you, Mom,
Beautiful and strong

killing me IS wrong!
Give me a chance!
Mam, don't leave me!
Mum, don't hurt me!
Mom, don't destroy me!
I WILL GIVE YOU A CHANCE!
I AM takes a loving glance
Mothers can forsake you!
I AM will not forsake you.

He dried up my tears

He dried up my tears,
when bitterness engulfed my heart
my soul tormented, hunted by a fiery
darts!
Reproach, disgrace and shame
were constant companions in
widowhood,
They clung to me like a knighthood,
isolated by all, choking, complaining
Soaked, drenched, weeping,
Wailing, "All is lost, all is gone!"
Suddenly I felt a gentle glow
His love surrounded me!
"Hush! Hush I AM is here!
It is Jehovah Shammar!"
He dried up my tears
when betrayal arose,
friends became enemies
families like foes!
Desertion, devastation, destruction,
encircled by frustration.
No way to turn!
Bawling, bewailing, bemoaning,
Bursting into tears in deep fear
"Nobody loves me! Nobody cares!"
Lamenting! Confused, faithless
Struggling in my distress and stress
His voice came as clear running water
"I will never leave you!"
It is Jehovah Nissi, my banner!
He dried up my tears,

when sickness rose
to torment my flesh
Headaches, neckaches, backaches.
Every nerve frailed!
Croaking, choking,
moaning and groaning!
The pain clung and refuse to leave!
Antibiotics, painkillers, tranquilizers
made a fertile bed in my abdomen
disfiguring mind body and soul.
Laying helplessly, groaning, moaning.
Mourning "Take me home
Lord! NOW!"
Closing my eyes, the final call!
He sent me His heartfelt Word!
"By my stripes you are healed!"
Instantly the chains broke!
I was free! Free to live!
It is Jehovah Rapha, my healer!
He dried up my tears!
When recession and depression
came to stay, my account
they nested and rested.
Given room to the twins,
inflation and deflation.
Prices rose, sky rocketed,
causing stagnation, damnation
Adding more hard and bad times.
Now in the red, so I buried my head!
Resided in bed, everything dead!
Can't pay the mortgage, can't rent!

No dosh for electric, gas or water bill!
No money, no food, gosh I feel ill!
Help! Is there a food bank?
Then I heard a whisper,
"Look to me, your helper!"
It is Jehovah Jireh my provider!

Let Him dry your tears!
Give Him all your fears!
In Sickness He heals!
In Pain He comforts!
When rejected you are His elect!
In weakness He gives Strength!
When poverty strikes He gives his riches!
In the pit, He pulls out of the ditch!
It is Jehovah El Shadai, Almighty God!

The mighty month of May

Oh mighty May full of grace!
The light of my Saviour's face,
He showed me His winning ways
Lengthened with strength my days.
In this spring month of May,
God gave the sun to make hay,
His peace streamed like a river
My mouth birthed a spoon of silver!
This miraculous month of May!
God's blessings came to stay
my dead state He raised to life
New song! New dance! No strive!
This marvellous month of May!
All my demons God did slay
with the blood of His only Son
my spirit set free, now reborn.
Oh mighty month of May!
Come again! Come to stay!
I promise not to go astray!
Giving thanks for each day.

Child soldier! Toy soldier!

Child soldier, toy soldier
He was caught in the game,
OH! what a shame
Who is to blame?
For this WAR! Rumours of WAR!
Fighting for a cause,
inspired from a distance far,
he is only thirteen, not yet eighteen!
Boy soldier, toy soldier!
So filled with hate,
I hope for his sake
we are not too late.
His country's burden upon his shoulder.
Don't you know these are only thirteen,
Not qualified till eighteen!
Child Soldier, toy soldier!
Already cursing, hating, killing,
fighting like mean men,
some are nine and ten.
scarred for life, like hen!
My friend this is no hype,
many are only thirteen,
Shouldn't they be eighteen?
Girl soldier, doll soldier!
abducted, gagged and beaten,
abused, molested then raped.
Hey, listen she is no ape.
Groped at fourteen,
Forced before she is eighteen.
Child soldier, toy soldier,
No Game Boy, No Nintendo.

No Ludo or even Cluedo,
Stolen Childhood,
Stolen dreams
darkened hearts,
Damned souls.
These are just thirteen,
Come on, they should be eighteen!
Child Soldier, toy soldiers!
lying in the trenches,
instead on the school benches
firing rocket propelled grenade,
instead of being at home drinking
cool-aid.
Some twelve, some thirteen
None of them are eighteen.
Child soldier, toy Soldier!
marching on Easter morn,
So cold, he wished he had not been
born,
mother and father gone.
Six feet under in a grave
he is so alone, in a darkened cave.
Run! Run! boy
to the foot of the cross.
Let God take the dross.
Lay your burdens down,
Peace! Sweet peace at last
He knows you're only thirteen,
and not yet eighteen.
Child Soldier! Toy soldier!
separated from friends

all around Him is that smell,
Yes! smoke, fire, the stench of HELL.
Surrounded by friends now dead,
life in these trenches he dreads.
Come my PEOPLE!
Sign the petition,
This is a new edition.
Awake from your slumber
let us erase this evil,
until all teens are safe in bed,
drinking milk and honey. Well fed!

The "Ifs" of God

If my people, my chosen people,
Whom I have called by my name,
Would resist the world
Read, believing my sacred words
Apply it in one accord,
Then I will part their Red Sea
And calm their storm.
I would visit them for all to see
That I AM, that I AM!
If my people whom I have,
Purchased with the blood of my Son,
Would not fear but walk by faith courage
Look to me and not be discouraged.
Then I would grant them grace and mercy,
Even in the famine they would not lack,
My people do not let your hand slack!
If my royal priesthood, my people whom I have,
Whom I brought out of deceit and darkness
Would their hearts harness,
And live by my statutes and precepts,
Then I would cause them to triumph.
Yes! Deliver them from all their woes,
By defeating all their foes!
If my people, the apple of my eyes.
Daily, would humble on their knees,
Fast, pray and praise before my throne,
stop the mutter, moan and drone.
And turn from their wicked ways,
Then, I will heal them and lengthen their days.
Because they are my turtle doves,
And in them, I will pour my love!

If my people whom I greatly delight
Upon whom I have set my sight,
Would obey my voice and follow,
And stop living a life of sorrow,
Then I would be their shepherd,
I would lead them as my sheep.
My Spirit would lead them out of the deep,
In peace, they would rest and sleep.

Printed in the United States
By Bookmasters